MW01532992

Dear God, Am I Important?

Dear God, Am I Important?

JAYNE BREMYER

WORD BOOKS, PUBLISHER
Waco, Texas

4301

Contents

Give Us This Day Our Daily Bread

Forgive Us Our Trespasses

As We Forgive Those Who Trespass against Us

Lead Us Not into Temptation

But Deliver Us from Evil

OUR FATHER
WHO ART IN HEAVEN

Dear Friend

I was going through a down cycle when I first wrote this private correspondence with God. I did it because there's something helpful about putting things down on paper. I figured I'd clarify my troubles so I could think better.

But what I didn't expect—what surprised me—was that after I wrote it down I not only knew the questions, I knew the answers too. Sometimes the problems just seemed to go away. Other times they simply didn't seem the same after I wrote them down, and I always got special new insights that helped me have a better perspective.

I told my friends how well this worked, and some of them started writing down their troubles and insights and addressing them to God. The same things happened to them.

Lucy wrote some of these letters to God, and they helped her to leave this life behind and move with faith into the next level, holding trustfully to God's hand.

11

My secretary, Sue, also wrote some. Her children were younger. Money was scarce. She ate compulsively, and her health was bad. Soon she also contracted cancer, but she received renewed faith and zest for life by writing down her thoughts. Keeping a journal changed her perspective toward her problems, and in the writing she received and wrote answers which God gave her. They helped her face the future valiantly. Sue recovered to go on to a full, meaningful life, knowing who she is and who God is.

I had problems with smoking, my daughter's rejection, my birthdays, and with intense fears and insecurities I'd had since my very unstable childhood. I was afraid of competition. I was afraid of pain, of club meetings, of death—of everything. Most of all I was afraid of going down the same path of so many women —clubs, little parties, widowhood, retirement homes, and burdening my children. I didn't know who I was or where I could go. But I wanted to be able to cope and depend on myself as a person, not on someone else.

A number of the other letters to God were written by women besides myself. No one has each and every one of these problems, at least not all at the same time. God never gives us more than we can bear if we turn our problems over to him. But all women have some of these situations. It's part of God's plan for our growth.

I gathered and edited these letters in the hope that those who contributed them might help you to accept yourself and know who you are and how God loves and plans for you. We hope they will encourage you to write in letter form your own private journal to God, your own personal thoughts and needs, knowing God will answer you too.

JAYNE BREMYER

HALLOWED BE THY NAME

To Lucy
*who wrote some of these letters while she
was dying of cancer, and who showed us that when
we know God has a plan and a will for us
that controls our lives, we can unite our will
with his*

THY WILL BE DONE

My Birthday

Dear God:

Today is my birthday. Time is running out. What have I really done? What have I accomplished?

My ego hurts as badly as my sense of worth. No one looks at me anymore. It seems just yesterday (maybe I imagined it) that people (men) would turn and look at me on the street. God, I liked it!

When I was younger, much younger, I felt so *important*. I felt pretty. I felt like I could do anything I really wanted to do badly enough. I felt as though the whole world was just waiting for me! I didn't doubt that I had both the personal aptitudes and the brains to accomplish whatever I set my mind to.

But now, I sometimes feel that I have accomplished nothing at all! And it's too late to hope I ever can.

God, help me to remember what I already know inside. Joy in life comes not so much from achievements as from faithfulness. Real self-satisfaction comes from knowing that I have tried as all your disciples must try. You have said you require nothing of us but to do justly, to love mercy, and to walk humbly with you. Help me remember that failure in an enterprise is not the same thing as failing as a person.

God, now that I am older, I have to regroup. I have to reevaluate my goals and take another look at my values. I used to think that to do something "great," to be very successful or important, would give some sort of immortality. But as my life has progressed, I see that there is no such thing as immortality in the eyes of the world (or my peers). Even the most important artists or writers or politicians and leaders are scarcely remembered a few weeks after they are gone from this level. (It must be very disillusioning, I've thought, for such people as presidents and leaders of worldwide importance to find that almost the day they're out of office their status changes from being the biggest top news to the "small print!")

The world is so vast, time is so unfathomably long, and people are so numerous. No matter what one does on this earth, it could only be a tiny drop on the sands of time.

The only important thing is to do each action, as unto you. In you we have our only immortality. Only that done for you will last.

So, all I want now is to do something useful, to do what I do well, and to be content, knowing that in you I will live forever.

JAYNE

"There is a right time for everything:
  A time to be born,
  A time to die" (Eccles. 3:2).

On Being Middle-Aged

Dear God:

The other day I overheard myself described as middle-aged.

Middle-aged! How can that be? But middle-aged must mean the middle of one's life! So, when I think of my life expectancy, I can't imagine that I am *not* middle-aged.

When I meet new people and ask how long they've been married or how old their children are (and it has been anywhere comparable to our years), I automatically think of them as being quite old and settled and unexciting. Much older than I. Yet actually—*I am the very same age!* The whole thing seems impossible. It seems only yesterday that John and I were first married and the children were small.

When I was young and going with John, I thought that to be able to live with him, to face him across the table at each meal, to spend almost every night with him, to sleep curled up in his arms each night, would be even more wonderful than a perpetual date with a license to enjoy, in sanctity, the most beautiful and intimate experiences. I thought it would be "heaven."

Sometimes, God, between diapers and tiredness, and bills and crosses we have borne together, I momentarily lost sight of the fact that it was "heaven." But as I look back now at the overall pattern, it has been just what I expected. And, God, I'm grateful.

Thank you for the opportunity to be your vessel with my husband and children. Thank you for the feel of your strength and for the opportunities to help you have given me. Thank you for my exceptional life. When I look back, I see you in everything. Who could ask for more?

Thank you, God, for the special circumstances of my life, and thank you too for the hard times. I see in them a special, tailor-made curriculum in which to learn from you the lessons of this earth experience. And you are the most tender and concerned of all loving teachers.

God, I've used up a lot of the years of my life, and for the most part the experiences have been joyous and fulfilling. But now I'm older, and I want back my used ration points so that I can hold on and live again.

In earth eyes this is impossible, too much to ask. Yet, God, I know with you nothing is impossible, and even this you will give me. As long as I make my free-will choice to stay with you, my talents will consistently be recharged and multiplied, and my life-cycles will constantly renew themselves.

JAYNE

"Everything is appropriate in its own time. But . . . man cannot see the whole scope of God's work from beginning to end" (Eccles. 3:11).

How Did I Get So Old?

Dear God:

How did I get so old?

I guess the only alternative would have been to die younger, and that I didn't want to do. But overnight, long before the time was due, here I am. I have half-grown children, and I can't be the age I think of myself as being, but the age that my children's ages indicate I must be. The *awful* age. In our society, no one is worth near as much old as young!

Still there would be some compensations if one could *feel* dignified and learned and *experienced* and have a sort of seniority. But, God, you know what? I have all the disadvantages of *being* older and none of the advantages of feeling secure and sure that are supposed to go with it. As a matter of (horrible) fact, I have discovered the older I am, the less sure I am!

But, God, in order to know myself, I must know you, and in order to know you, I must lose myself. My consciousness of self (age, looks, ego, self-will, and desires) stands between me and knowing. This sense of self and separation in me is represented by the Devil because it keeps me from knowing, understanding, and picturing myself as I really am. My self-centeredness hides my real identity so I don't know my togetherness with each separate person, and I don't realize all I have is yours, Father.

You have said, "Lo, I am with you alway, even unto the end of the world." And, "Though you take the wings of the morning and fly to the uttermost parts of the sea, even there I am with you." "Where can you go to escape my vigil?"

I know this isn't an intellectual quest. On the contrary, it is anti-intellectual. Intellect stands in the way. And if I try to go about understanding only with my head, I get all hung-up because I'm operating on a different frequency.

I must know who I am. If I don't know, I won't picture myself accurately. I'll go on forever feeling cut off —too old, too unimportant, too lacking in confidence and afraid, orphaned and unsure.

God, help me understand who I am. Let me see myself as you see me. In your eyes, I am the real me! Age and time and outward appearance have nothing to do with me as I am with you.

JAYNE

❧

"Whatever is, has been long ago; and whatever is going to be has been before; God brings to pass again what was in the distant past and disappeared" (Eccles. 3:15).

My Child
Doesn't Like Me Anymore

O God:

My daughter doesn't like me. She told me so. I have loved her so much, too much. With an overwhelming intensity I have wanted for her whatever she wanted for herself. Too late now I see that I have spoiled her. I have failed her if she is self-centered.

Still, I'm sorry for myself. It doesn't seem fair that I should hurt like this for my good intentions. But no mother should hope to balance the ledger between the love she gives and gets in the same generation. Mothers (and fathers) have their own debts to repay to the parents of their youth, whose love-ledger was never balanced fairly. It is inevitable that children take more from us than they give and repeat the cycle by giving more to their own children than they can ever get. Father, I know this is your pattern for continuing life and love.

My too-much beloved and indulged daughter has been so much emulated by me. Oh, God, I've made mistakes, a real mess of things. I've been so proud of

27

her that I've been absolutely unable to keep quiet about her charms and accomplishments. I should have known that my bragging and open pride were annoying her and my friends. But I so wanted everyone to think that we were close that I bragged shamefully. I verbally clutched at any straw to make it look as if we shared ever so many things.

The truth is it's been so long since she was like I picture her that I can scarcely remember the sweet little-girl trust and dependence. Ever since that long-ago time Jill has been hell-bent on cutting the umbilical cord as well as any other emotional ties and connections with me. She seems barely to tolerate me. Almost every look and action from her indicates more clearly than volumes of words an "oh, mother!" attitude of disdain. She is conscientiously uncommunicative, and she is resentful. The more I love her, the worse she treats me.

I wish I could still manage to believe I am super-sensitive and that I imagine at least a bit of this. But, God, I can't even do this any longer. When I insisted she bring her thoughts out in the open, she confirmed all my suspicions.

This year-in-year-out long, long delivery of my girl child from my heart and home is much harder than it was to deliver her from my body. For a mother, this labor with a daughter seems much more difficult than with the boys. A daughter is a special tie to a mother. She is an extension of more than her body. She is like a tangible incarnation of both her will and her wishes. When anything happens to a daughter, it is as though it also happened to her mother because a mother can understand almost too well each thing her girl child goes through. So much have I been at one with her hopes and dreams for herself (in my own hopes and plans) that I have even felt through her feelings.

So you see, this hurts clear through, Lord, more than anything has ever hurt, more than any physical pain could penetrate.

God, as Jill told me how deeply she resented me, my commitment to you made me think of Saint Francis. What experiences taught him his creed? Lessons don't come easy in this world, even to saints. I managed to tell my grown-up and grown-away girl that it was more important to me to give than to get and to help than to be helped and to love than to be loved. If I could help her become a good person, it was secondary how she felt about me personally.

I was proud I could get it out. But, God, give me strength that when my lips say this, my heart can mean it. When I said it, I thought my heart would break, and I didn't take this stoically with nothing in my mind and heart but "giving" as Saint Francis might have managed to do. As she went blithely off with her boyfriend, untouched by the anguish she knew I felt, I cried myself sick!

God, if I must cry, please let me cry only real tears and not any extra for self-pity!

God, I want to ask you to forgive her and help her because maybe she can't help how she feels about me at this stage of growing up and becoming independent. (Maybe she never will like me again!) But she knew how torn apart I was, and she did nothing, or said nothing, to ease my pain. In this I'm not only sorry for myself; I'm concerned for her that, as an evolving soul, she may end up selfish and thoughtless. Regardless of her resentments, someday when she is a mother, I think she may be sorry she stood by and watched, unmoved, the suffering she has been instrumental in causing.

She may have to suffer for her insensitivity because under the law that we reap what we sow, she will have to learn. And, God, I don't want any lessons to come too hard for her or at too great a price. If she is actually as insensitive as she seems, I'm really afraid for her.

Yet maybe I am the insensitive one. Is it possible that she is sorry already and doesn't know how to express it? Maybe she can't get her feelings together so they come out right. I mean this need to separate herself from me and still show some kindness or maybe even love.

If she doesn't love me (or can't), it is bound to hurt her, maybe even more than it hurts me, because she is an extension of me and there is no way she can change her heritage. She can't feel comfortable. She can't feel right about herself if she can't clarify her feelings.

But most of all, God, I ask you to make *me* remember that you are all-powerful and all-good. You have a plan. I have put myself in your will and subjected myself to your plan, and I've put my daughter there too. I believe that she too has placed herself in your will and care. I believe she wants to belong to you as much as I do. So nothing can happen to us ultimately that is not part of your plan. We could not contest your will about the lessons or hard cycles we must go through in order to grow spiritually.

Apparently it is your will that almost all parents and children go through hard feelings of separation in order that children might emerge from the home-nest strong and independent and able to fly on their own wings. (And when they do, they fly back to the nest. At least in their hearts.) Bless my daughter's flight.

And bless parents too. Especially mothers must learn that there comes a time when we must shut the door on what is past and open new doors of our own independence and interests, with only you to guide us into brand-new and untried areas of service.

So, Lord, I ask your blessing on both my daughter and me. Bless us as we travel our separate ways. And please, God, if it be in your will for us, I hope we can come again to travel together once in awhile. Maybe this can happen when she's in college or has a home and a child of her own. I want her to know I will always be here, waiting.

Please, God, give us strength and wisdom and the necessary courage for this hard, complex, and confusing relationship that happens between half-grown daughters and too-dependent mothers.

But most of all, whatever life might hold, I claim your promise and will for both of us. I know you will keep us together always, at least in our commitment to your will, your plan, and your love.

JAYNE

✿

"Teach a child to choose the right path, and when he is older he will remain upon it" (Prov. 22:6).

God,
I've Got to Learn to Live
with Loneliness

Dear God:

These days I don't want to get up. I've been having a terrible time facing the day. Now that there is nothing to get up for, what am I to do? How can I keep going with any enthusiasm now that the children are gone and my husband so seldom home? The whole empty day alone, with no one who really needs me, just seems too much, God.

Dear Lord, give me the insight to know that somewhere in this day or in the days ahead you have an important place for me in your plan. Perhaps I will be unaware of these moments. Still, Lord, I know that as long as I am on this earth, I am important in your plan, or you would take me off this earth.

I *can* live creatively, finding new and worthwhile joys in the future. "The best is yet to be," said Robert Browning. I know this is true. Like Paul, I can forget those things that are behind and strain toward that which lies ahead. I know I can run without fainting when I run in your will, when I soar ahead to fill your jobs and purposes.

JAYNE

❧

"If you love your father and mother more than you love me, you are not worthy of being mine; or if you love your son or daughter more than me, you are not worthy of being mine. If you refuse to take up your cross and follow me, you are not worthy of being mine" (Matt. 10:37–38).

I Don't Want
to Ask Too Much

Dear Father:

I think I have been guilty of grabbing and gobbling at life and of trying to control my own life rather than giving it to you. I should have complete trust and absolute gratitude for what you have given. Instead, I've often put myself and my human needs above my love for you. I haven't accepted your intervening care with gratitude. I've scarred your plan and gift by lacking total faith and by my human desire for more and more. I've so much to be grateful for—husband, family, kids, past experiences and opportunities, special jobs. You continually give me people to help as well as material things, so much of everything. But, still, I've wanted more.

God, you know what I've really coveted. I've wanted to be all things to all people, and I've wanted to have even more love from those who already love me. I have wanted the intelligence, career success, wit, talents, popularity, and social position of everyone. I've coveted everyone else's life rather than finding contentment in being what you made me, in being myself. I haven't been satisfied. Forgive me, and help me see my failings so that I might recover from them. Help me to be willing to accept me.

God, I believe you have wanted to give me special work for you. You've controlled my life and my circumstances so that I see this purpose to such an extent that I believe nothing can happen outside your will. So I'm no longer afraid. Even if death is your will for me, I can accept it. But, Father, I want to live while I live. No one can live life as a captive of death.

Help me, dear Father, to try again with fresh determination. Help me to give myself altogether into your hands and to give back to you what you've given me. I want to give back each person, each day, each joy, and whatever talent you've loaned me. I want to be worthy in your sight and strong and able all the days I live. I need to find the opportunities you've given to me. I must turn out of me that which is inside my life. I have to do this to love, and I have to do your will to be of service to you because to love is my life.

JAYNE

❧

"But God showed his great love for us by sending Christ to die for us while we were still sinners" (Rom. 5:8).

36

Lord,
I Hate
My Self-Centeredness

Father:

My personality bugs me. My hang-ups bug me. Today I know, Father God, how weak and small I really am! I'm so unimportant that the fact itself bothers me. I'm hung up because I'm not witty or accomplished. I seem to have zero poise or sophistication. As a matter of fact, I'm just plain "different" from other people. I despise being different, and I'm not clever or even very smart.

But, Father, no matter how true this is, what worries me more is that it should make me, your child, *feel* unimportant. The real problem is the shame I feel when I have a much greater gift. How I appear in worldly ways shouldn't worry me at all, one way or another. It proves that, except for your investment of love in me, I truly am insignificant. What shattering proof of my underdeveloped spiritual state! I'm shocked to realize that I still think such worldly things matter, even after you have taught me who I really am. What a discouraging realization that where it really counts I actually am inadequate. Inadequate spiritually! This must be true, or I wouldn't care about superficial appearances.

Father, I am ashamed that, even for a minute, I could think that such considerations would count with me. I've known all along I was nothing of myself. Still, I am as important as anyone who ever lived. But I know my importance is through you because you love me.

It must be insulting to you beyond all hurts that I (or anyone) could discount so easily your love. Obviously you love me specially, and you've shown me so in every way. God, I just can't believe me! How can I be concerned about the things that worry me when, in spite of being outright self-centered and choked with earthly fear of being different, I know I'm still everything with you? My self-centeredness is pure conceit.

Father, I guess if my sins were glamorous, active ones (like shocking immoral things), I'd see them for what they are. Sins of the heart are just as bad as these obvious kinds, and sometimes I think they might be even worse. My burdens of feeling wrong are all tied up with mundane negatives like what I *don't* do and what I *don't* appreciate. This gives me the terrible feeling of being nothing. I haven't done any awful thing so that you can love me like a prodigal daughter. I'm more like an older daughter who stays home and does nothing except be guilty of what she doesn't do, doesn't realize, doesn't appreciate.

I'm dense, insensitive, and slow to understand. How this must hurt you. Except for you in me, I feel sure today that I really haven't progressed at all. Of myself I'm still weak and nothing.

Paul said a mouthful when he wrote, "Lucky is he who has no reason to judge himself." Please, Father, take away my reasons.

JAYNE

"Let everyone be sure that he is doing his very best, for then he will have the personal satisfaction of work well done, and won't need to compare himself with someone else. Each of us must bear some faults and burdens of his own. For none of us is perfect!" (Gal. 6:4–5).

I Can't Forget
How Old and Bad I Look

Dear God:

What good looks you gave me surely don't seem to be with me anymore. I've *hated* the deepening vertical lines that have formed between my eyes. I've *despised* the bags under them, and I couldn't stand my glasses. The soft, puffy flab beneath my chin (that no sort of high-neck clothes seem to hide) has been absolutely devastating, and my frizzy thinning hair is disgusting.

God, lately I've hardly been able to forget my appearance for a moment. I've been humiliated by the changes taking place in me. They don't seem to be me!

The other day an elderly lady in a store asked me, "Have you got your glasses, dear? I can't see the price tag." For a moment I wondered, "How'd she know I need glasses in order to see price tags?" Then, with a shock, I realized she knew because I looked *that* age. In spite of all my careful, time-consuming camouflage, age was eating away on me like a cancerous growth, and there was no way to hide it. Even a half-blind lady could see it!

Every day my skin, face and body seem to deteriorate at a more accelerated pace. How much harder this is to accept than I ever thought it would be. I never would have believed I could get so conscious of my appearance or vain enough to care obsessively. Sometimes, God, I've even cared desperately! I couldn't seem to help running to the mirror each morning to see what new disaster had taken place, and I couldn't feel comfortable with the image that came back at me. My eyes shot like magnets to spots I knew looked the worst. I'd be so sick and disgusted I could cry! I wanted to tear off my sagging flesh or have a face-lift. Anything rather than go through the rest of my life hating my appearance and not looking the way I used to.

In my second adolescence I was like a teenager. I'd no idea how to adjust my personality to my age. And I found myself pleading, "God, who am I?"

While I was enduring these tortures, it seemed that every day my ridges got deeper and my sagging and crinkling skin was more impossible to ignore. Bitterly I asked, "Why do I have to get old quicker than other women my age?" When I passed a window or mirror, my eyes had compulsions of their own to nit-pick the telltale signs—the wrinkles, ridges, lines, and sagging chin. God, it just about made me hate myself. I told myself, "I can't go anywhere. I'll run into someone who hasn't seen me lately!" I felt sure that when anyone didn't utter the obvious social amenities, like, "How well you look," it was a certain sign that what he or she really meant was, "How awful you look!"

Well, God, these feelings just got worse and worse.

But one day I made up my mind that enough is enough! I figured I'd been compiling my troubles to where I not only hated my looks, I hated my thoughts, and I hated myself. So I decided to face facts. I couldn't put my mind out to others as you wanted me to when I was trapped in me. Any extreme self-consciousness, like thinking intensely about me and my mind and physical workings, is bound to bring on a crash. You told us not to turn our eyes—or our light—inwards, because then we can't see spiritually. You don't want us to hide our "light under a bushel." And I sure could burn myself doing it!

Well, God, I made up my mind not to let my feelings bolt out of control. And you know what? When I turned this degrading problem over to you, thoughts came to me that changed my attitude completely about losing my battle to hold onto youthful looks. The ideas just came (which I think of as "angel thoughts" since I'm sure they come from a higher level—from you and my guardian angels). They really did free me of my inner prison of self-consciousness.

So I'm writing down these insights so I won't ever get stuck in that sort of self-trap again. Putting them down will make them clearer and make me remember. God, I need to keep your answers close because they're the most valuable possessions I have, my protection against the lower part of me.

Though I'd wanted so much still to be "pretty," you arranged things so that I was made to remember that real beauty comes from the inside and radiates outward. For some reason I confided my concern to my daughter and daughter-in-law—maybe because they're still young and beautiful. Father, you know I don't believe in coincidences anymore, but their answers really amazed me. I know such helpful statements that someone seemingly makes by chance aren't just "chance" remarks. Chance is your pseudonym.

My daughter-in-law reminded me that when a woman is young she really can't be beautiful, no matter what she looks like. She said, "This is because she hasn't had time to develop real signs of character in her face. When you look at her, you only see outside." She reminded me that only time and experience can penetrate the mask of smooth skin and pierce the impenetrable eyes of youth so that the real light of a woman can shine through.

God, when she said this, I was reminded of a girl (well, "woman" would be a more accurate description) I know. She's older than I am, but she has no lines. From an early age she's held her face immobile, in a sort of dead-pan mask, empty of expression. She said she did this so she wouldn't have lines in her face! Also, I've another friend who has incredibly few of these tell-tale lines. People envy her, but I know she's paid a price. She's spent years of time-consuming care, and she's been so conscious of her looks that she's lost much of the love and respect of her husband. Wow! I think I'm glad I'm me, lines and all. I sure wouldn't change places with either of these gals!

And, God, I also want to remember what my daughter "chanced" to say. She said, "The first place anyone looks at another person is the eyes." I thought of how the eyes of a young person compare with eyes of older people. Older eyes often have a much more revealing beauty.

When I meet another woman, I'm a bit conscious of her physical appearance—at first. But when I talk to her, my impression of her switches almost immediately to my reactions to her more intangible qualities. Even in a brief encounter, my idea of what she's like is ever so much colored by her eyes, her deeper personality, her animation—or lack of it—her thoughts and attitudes. I've often realized it's only taken minutes to get an entirely different impression of her "appearance." The impression people make on one another goes all together in one package; it just doesn't come through an appraisal of this or that separate detail.

Other people besides me surely look deeper than physical imperfections for their idea of what a woman "looks like." People don't see other people just as physical, and they don't see specific signs of aging. Only the overall image registers.

Also, my beautiful daughter said, "Mom, you're being downright ridiculous to think that everyone who looks at you is thinking about your neck or is conscious of some specific feature about you."

She's right. This is conceit. How could I really think anyone would be *that* perceptive about anything about me anyway? Besides, most women I know are much too concerned about their own looks and the impression they're making to be conscious about specific flaws in someone else.

She said, "Mom, being young involves lots more than the texture of your skin. It depends on your whole attitude. Some people are always old. And others aren't old—ever!"

God, I know that, but I guess I just needed someone to remind me, and you sent someone.

I also know something else. If I really wanted to, I could pray for you to make me ageless. You can do anything, and if I have enough faith, you can do anything for me. You can reverse the ravages of time on a body the same as you reverse the course of cancer. But now, I realize, I don't really want this. I wouldn't want to spend my years and not have any trace of the time and experience on me. Especially since, with you, my years, my time, and my experience have been joyful. I want my face to show what's inside me.

Thank you, God, for the way things are. I don't really want anything different. I know you're all-powerful and that your plan controls all things. I don't want anything but your plan in my life. All I was thinking about was keeping a youthful prettiness. I forgot for a while that maturity brings real beauty.

Dear God, help me to be beautiful in ways that *really* count. May my appearance show the marks of tranquil, secure Christian faith and inner joy. I know it does because all that is there in me, and you shine through me. You'll always make me radiant.

Thank you, God.

JAYNE

❧

"*Men judge by outward appearance, but I look at a man's thoughts and intentions*" (1 Sam. 16:7).

I Have to Accept the Fact
That I'm Different

God:

Someone suggested that happiness comes from trusting people when there's no reason. But you know something, God? I think my happiness has to come from
trusting myself, even when I can't think of any good
reasons. Still, I'm finding out I have to respect me, and
to do this, I have to accept me. Otherwise I'm no good
for myself. If I'm not content inside, I can't serve you or
anybody.

But, Father, the trouble is sometimes I'm not sure
I've got any reasons to like and accept me, or even that
I should. Sometimes I'd be ever so pleased to be somebody else, but the Bible says you can tell the difference between what's good and bad by the "fruits."
And all the "good fruits" seem to come from people who
first like and accept their own personalities, proclivities,
and limitations. I want to be among the producers of
"good fruit." So such things as I can't change about me,
I want to accept.

God, I'm "different" because I'm a nonconformist. I

have no natural inclination toward "convention." Without a real unnatural effort, I don't fit into society and its mores. I feel differently about things than most people. I think differently. No matter how I try to hide it, what's inside me just keeps bulging out. I don't have the inhibitions and hang-ups society and convention are supposed to put on you "for your own protection." Also, Father, I feel things with a scary intensity. I wear my heart on the outside, and I've no armor to protect myself from the marksmanship of other people.

But, God, I've lived so long now without learning the things society is supposed to teach that I just have to give up trying to scrunch into the social mold. For me, it would be a strait jacket. I couldn't breathe or budge, and I'd be constantly ill at ease and squashed. I can't live that way.

Father, even though all this is true, sometimes I hurt with the idea of being "different." People aren't supposed to be different. When you're different, you aren't acceptable to lots of folks. You don't fit in lots of places.

You know, God, that I can't live my whole life self-conscious. If I do, I can't turn my feelings out to anyone else, like you want me to. So, I've asked your help, and now I know you've answered me. You always do. Your insights always come through when I ask with enough faith and when I thank you for knowing what's best and making things the way you have. I see now, I've wasted enough of your time—and mine—worrying about being different.

First, it came to me that all of us on this earth have to be "human." We're bound to be influenced by "mass consciousness." If we aren't normal according to scales and charts, then we're considered abnormal. Deviation from the mass code of conventions, which is supposed to be civilization's safeguard, is mistrusted. People don't understand, and they don't trust what they don't understand. They're afraid of "differentness." It's safer to run in packs. I guess I'm afraid too. Society makes you "feel wrong" whether or not you're wrong for your own individual self. Convention puts on the pressure by giving you the notion that wandering off from pack leaders is some sort of crime and that you'll have to go it alone if you do.

When a person's individualistic enough, or secure enough, inside or through you, to move about on faith without guidelines, he or she is bound to be made to feel different. But everyone is different in some way to some extent in some secret place inside, and everyone is scared of that difference. We're all scared of our own hidden secrets and of being found out. God, I reckon I'm not alone in being frightened when I see myself as "different." But you said that the world looks at how things seem and that you look at the heart.

You make all your children different and individualistic. You don't want us to be like sheep or cattle. You don't expect us to be alike. We don't need to feel pressured into alikeness in order to be secure. We all have different urges and reactions and thoughts and feelings. You made us this way; so I know you wanted us this way.

You've accepted us just like we are; you even loved us when we were "yet sinners," so we should love ourselves. God, it's still true that sometimes I can't help but wish I were a different me, and the way I think and feel isn't the whole of it. I wish I could look different, and sometimes I most certainly and surely wish my abilities and talents were different. But I just have to accept me—my personality, my looks, and my limitations.

God, I don't always want to be zeroing in on the idea you like me, or maybe I really need to understand how much you like me and then I'll just automatically like myself.

God, I don't always want to be zeroing in on the idea of what you can do for me. I want to be free to think of what I could maybe do for you, how to let you come through me. Please help me not to get carried away with what I'm not and what I can't do or can't be. Help me to know what and who I am and what I *can* do and *can* be—and to like what I see!

I thank you for the way things are—right now. God, if you like me—and I know for sure you do—then that's good enough for me! I guess I can safely like myself without being too far wrong. Thank you, God, that I'm me—after all.

JAYNE

❧

"When the Holy Spirit controls our lives he will produce this kind of fruit in us: love, joy, peace, patience, kindness, goodness, faithfulness, gentleness and self-control" (Gal. 5:22–23).

Please Tell Me Who I Am

Dear God:

There is so much noise in the world. Sometimes everything seems so outer-oriented that I really have to make an effort to hear and know the inside of me. So after I tell you what I need to say, God, I must hold very, very still and make my mind very still so I can close out all the outer things. Then I will know your voice and you will come through to me.

Feeling your presence is different from feeling anyone else's. Sometimes, God, when I try to feel someone else whom I love, in order to know his vibration and remember his look and the sound of his voice, his image escapes me. But I can always feel you. The minute I turn to you, there you are, so clear and close and near that all at once I tingle with the creative knowing of you, telling me you are within me.

Telling me who I am.

LUCY

✤

"What does the Lord your God require of you except to listen carefully to all he says to you, and to obey for your own good the commandments I am giving you today, and to love him, and to worship him with all your hearts and souls?" (Deut. 10:12–13).

ON EARTH AS IT IS
IN HEAVEN

The Choices I Make

Dear God:

"May the meditations of my mind be acceptable in thy sight." I ask it over and over, God, but still, they aren't. I'm at a crossroads, not only at a turning point in what paths I take, but also in which attitudes I choose. The things I do seem determined by how I feel about whether the thing is wrong or right. Everything I do—or don't do—has a cost, and I decide if it is worth the cost on the basis of what I really want.

I want most of all to do what you want me to do, but I don't know how I should feel. I don't know for sure what is right and what is wrong in your eyes. It's difficult to know without a true direct line to you because there don't seem to be as many signs along the road (mores and customs) for guidance.

Again and again I haven't considered what was your will. Before I realized it, I was in the miserable state of being separated in my mind from you. Other times I've thought I made the right choice, but I've been wrong because the results were wrong. We are free to make our own choices, but it seems we never get free of the choices we make.

My goodness, God, you'd think after so many times I'd be like a burned child and I'd not make the same mistakes again, that I'd be able to claim the promises you have made. I want to let the mind of Christ be in me as you promised it could be. If I would seek, you said I'd find. And when I knock, you promised you would open the door.

God, help me. I love you and you love me. All I need do to receive your gifts and realize your promises is to ask. And I ask. When I have decisions to make, show me which choices are right. And since I know you'll do this because I asked, thank you, God.

JAYNE

❧

"I have told you all this so that you will have peace of heart and mind. Here on earth you will have many trials and sorrows; but cheer up, for I have overcome the world" (John 16:33).

Help Me Never
to Start Smoking Again

God:

Something has changed with me, and the change was totally beyond my power. Miraculously you have helped me overcome my years of slavery to smoking. Again and again I have put down my intentions and confessions in letters to you—like this one:

Right now it seems to me that the most wonderful words in the world would be, "No, thank you. I don't smoke." I want to be free of smoking. I've thought it all out, and here's why:

It's a burden that interferes with other commitments—prayer, my husband, my work, kids, reading. Smoking is an illusive coping device that's become a constant worry and a drag. It robs me of joy and freedom and answers nothing.

From numerous too-real experiences, I know that I hate everything about smoking—the cough, the smell, the sore throats, the dirtiness, the pains in my chest, the phlegm in my throat, the stopped-up sinuses, the constant need and its control over me. Smoking endangers my health. Everyone with any sense nowadays knows this.

I can't visualize myself facing any and all situations without the need to clutch a cigarette for support. If I have to use patience in solving a problem, if there is no action I can take, it crosses my mind, "I have to have a cigarette."

Help me, God, to quit smoking.

Finally, you came through to me. If I was ever really to quit smoking, I had to stop rationalizing, examine the symptoms, and get at the source of my trouble. Then, clearly, the source occurred to me: I had not completely given over all circumstances to you. I resolved to make amends immediately.

Now I do all things, including *not* smoking, through you and in your strength. I can cope with anything and I am self-sufficient—in your power. I don't worry about questions or how to resolve personally some situation I don't know how to handle. If I wait with patience, God, you come through.

Thank you—again, again, and again!

JAYNE

❧

"Haven't you yet learned that your body is the home of the Holy Spirit God gave you, and that he lives within you? Your own body does not belong to you. For God has bought you with a great price. So use every part of your body to give glory back to God, because he owns it" *(1 Cor. 6:19–20).*

I'm a Compulsive Eater

Dear God:

I have such an unworthy problem that I'm embarrassed to tell you about it. Yet I know you're looking at me; so there's no way to hide. God, I'm a compulsive eater.

I look at myself and think of all the times I've vowed to lose those extra pounds, and I *know* I want to stop eating. I know you're able to keep me from doing things that are not your will, and overeating can't be your will for me. But the real problem is me. Do I really want to ask your help? Maybe I'd just rather have that piece of cake.

I visualize what it would be like to be down to a petite size again instead of all this extra flab and bulk. I feel like a Jonah who swallowed the whale rather than the other way around. I *know* I don't want to eat—ever again. "I'll never eat more than just enough to stay alive," I tell myself. To be slim again would be worth anything!

After all, what's the big deal about declining an extra doughnut or buttered toast or potatoes? And ice cream is such a small thing. Within seconds it's all devoured, and I have years to regret it. I regret it when I go to buy a new dress. I regret it even more when my friends Tammy and Peg slink into the room in their tight pants. I tell myself it isn't ladylike to show off their figures like they do. (But, God, you and I know, if that's being unladylike, at heart I'm no "lady" myself!) I think I'll go and buy clothes exactly like theirs, but when the picture of me in their clothes slides across my inner vision, I know it takes more than clothes to make the woman. I know for sure it would be worthwhile to pass by all goodies when I see how Howard looks at Tammy. Father, I think it's true what they say about "it's better to be looked over than overlooked." Being overlooked makes you feel so terribly unimportant.

But, God, when I tell myself these things, it isn't dinnertime! And that's the trouble! Someone passes the food, and I'm off again.

Sometimes I make excuses. (Just a snitch of calories off someone's plate or the hole from the middle of the doughnut doesn't count.) But sometimes I don't even bother to make excuses! I just deliberately block out the warning gong. Oh, God, right when I reach for that piece of candy is when I need to do my praying, when I need your help. And if I don't ask, how can I expect it? Help me to ask at the right times! Don't let me cop out because I know you would answer my prayer and I'd rather have that piece of cake.

Dear God, help me to remember (at the temptation times) that you say our bodies are your temple. I don't want my wondrous gift of your presence to be encased in an ugly shell. I want your home in me to be beautiful —and healthy.

God, help me to want this more than that extra piece of cake.

Sue

"Many others have faced exactly the same problems before you. . . . You can trust God to keep the temptation from becoming so strong that you can't stand up against it, . . . He will show you how to escape temptation's power" *(1 Cor. 10:13).*

May I Not Focus on Material Things

God:

Help me, I pray, to keep from centering myself around earthly things. Such pretenses give me the most awful sense of sin imaginable. I'm sure that "sin" is not what people generally think at all, but an attitude of mind and an emphasis on material things. So often I feel guilty. I detest in me and dislike in my loved ones the compulsion to depend for comfortableness on such things as cigarettes and drink or any sort of worldly prop.

O Father, if I could just rise above the uncomfortableness or sense of lostness that makes me feel that I must press toward something or that I lack something or need to hold on to something for support. If only I could disassociate myself from the compulsion to look for this support from the next drink, the next meal, snack, cigarette—or even from a cup of coffee! If I could "press on toward the goal of the high calling of God" along with the apostle Paul.

Father God, help me to *realize* that you are *all*, everything that is. You can give those who ask the living water that satisfies.

JAYNE

🌽

"Don't worry about things—food, drink, and clothes. For you already have life and a body—and they are far more important than what to eat and wear" (Matt. 6:25).

GIVE US THIS DAY OUR
DAILY BREAD

Lord,
Bless These Flights of Fancy

Dear God:

If I had become a doctor, I'd have found a cure for cancer by now.

Evidently the world isn't ready for that, or I'd be Dr. Maiden Name Jones instead of Mrs. Cook - maid - chauffeur - laundress - ironing-lady - gardener - hair-stylist - barber - bookkeeper - mistress - etc. Smith.

Yes, sir, the world would certainly have been a better place had I been Dr. Jones instead of Mrs. Smith!

Maybe? Just a little, maybe?

Well, I didn't, and I'm not, and it isn't (in that order).

So, God, what have you planned exciting for me today? Cook? Good. I'll bake a pie and turn on the oven light and watch the meringue turn brown. Laundry? Here's my chance to expand my mind and keep up with chemistry. Bleach. Enzymes. Fabric softener. Wash and wear. Stain-resistant. Bookkeeper? I used the last of the red pencil yesterday. Is there no end to this perpetual round of gaiety?

Lord, had I become Dr. Jones, I'd have been in medical school instead of behind that desk where I met Howard. I'd have been given a diploma instead of a son and a successful experiment instead of my daughter.

I am content.

Thank you for these flights of fancy and fits of frustration. They keep me emotionally stable. They remind me that I care for what I am and what I have. It comes from you.

SUE

❦

"You are the world's seasoning, to make it tolerable. If you lose your flavor, what will happen to the world?" (Matt. 5:13).

Something More than Housework

Dear God:

I've wanted to be a "person" in my own right, with something to do beyond being mother and wife or a nameless someone without a separate personality to call my own. I've always wanted my own special individualism, a specific job outside my family unit that I could put a part of myself into. My family's needs must be your first will for me and should be the most important opportunity I have to express myself. But, even so, I've rationalized that in making a place for myself outside our home I will be able to give my family wider horizons. (Actually, God, was I thinking of wider horizons for my family or for me?)

It has seemed that there were so few ways to show my personal touch or gain insight into the world around me by doing housework! Sometimes it has seemed that there are no ways at all for the ordinary housewife to be original. How I hate those words. Housework! Housewife! (I'm not a wife of this house!)

As you see, God, I've been feeling dissatisfied and

jealous that in other work there seem to be so many more creative and original possibilities.

I've been thinking a lot about this, God, but now it seems that you are telling me I was wrong to get all bugged and "uptight" over this. If I look, there really are ways to show my individuality (and yours) in "our" loving labor for my family. If I stay aware, I can demonstrate that the things I do for people are done with that special love you've inspired in me. It's possible to do my family work as though I were doing it for you!

Help me, Father, to think of ways to put my personal signature (and yours) on what I do so my home will show evidences that love has been at work.

Maybe it can come through in keeping clean towels on the shelves so my children won't have to run to the dryer for one, or paying special attention when I put socks away so my husband can pull out a pair first try without pulling out everything in the drawer.

I need to find the *extra* things to do. I want to do more than just see that the flowers have cool, fresh water to drink. I need to put "me" into the way they are arranged. (God, I hope you'll help me to do this with enough love to make up for my lack of competency.)

I want to do my work well enough so our home will show the special care that will make my husband and children feel love and peace when they are here and carry with them warm memories of home to make them secure when they are away.

At least, Father, I realize now that everyone keeps house differently. And homes do (or should) mirror the tastes and talents and the interests and individual-

70

ity of the people who live there. The mother and wife lives there most of all; so she sets the scene.

Please keep me open, God, to creative ways to show the special precious individuality of each person who lives here. Help me make the love I feel for each person a tangible thing.

One of the warmest feelings I'll ever remember was the day Darla's friend came home after school with her. She told me she wished her mother would learn to knit so she would make her a vest. Her mother always bought things. After her friend left, Darla put her arms around me and gave me a big hug. She didn't say what it was for, but I knew.

Thank you, God, for bringing this back to the top of my memory.

God, you can help me to see more possibilities in the way I fix our food (maybe cake decorating lessons would give me a chance outside the home to mix with people), and even a special way of setting the table and serving meals. (What courses is the Extension Office offering now?) And maybe I can also show it in the special care I give ironing, and in such things as originality in decorating our home and in giving thought to each member's individual preferences.

It seems to me now, God, that our home can (and maybe already does) show the quality and quantity of my love and your love too. I feel happier and more satisfied.

You can continue to help me maintain this home and be a good mother and wife in a way that can materialize that special spring of creativity that wells up inside me in my love for you—also in my love for those others that are mine through you.

I want to serve you through serving my family. This is your will for me.

SUE

❧

"So he got up from the supper table, took off his robe, wrapped a towel around his loins, poured water into a basin, and began to wash the disciples' feet and to wipe them with the towel he had around him" (John 13:4-5).

I Feel So Unimportant

Dear God:

Today I feel terribly unimportant. My husband woke up full of plans and purposes for his day, joyfully looking forward to everything. The kids raced out the door smelling of fresh skin, sprays, and lotions. Their day is crammed full of tests and challenges and chats in the halls.

I went back to my coffee and paper, but all the time I was wondering how I would keep up my spirits during a long silent day empty of everything but household duties and preparations for the return of the chiefs. God, sometimes I get so tired of being the Indian.

And yet, God, another part of me clutches the compensating fact that there are several chiefs in my home instead of one because I know it won't be long until they are all gone, except for the big chief. The children will leave, bubbling with plans, and I will stay behind and see them only occasionally. Eventually I will realize that we are no longer their first family, though they will always be ours. I know I should treasure every minute of these few last fleeting years while they are still home.

But, God, I need to feel important myself. I need to put my own personal ambition somewhere. I sometimes think I don't want to be the hub of the wheel with all the spokes of the family grinding in on me. (Or could this idea be a defense mechanism? Maybe I want to fool myself, leave them emotionally before they leave me.) But what I'm thinking now, God, is that I want to be me, somebody special in my own right.

Yet, God, I have always asked to be a vessel. Back a million years ago when I was master of my fate, my choice was to be used. Obviously we should be careful what we ask. We will get it. I've asked, and I do want to be a vessel. I do! I really do! Oh, God, help me not to chicken out when the going gets tough or down to the nitty gritty.

After all, if I were an end in myself, I would use all my talent and my special gifts and not pass them on to my children. Even when it seems to me that all my kids are much smarter than I, part of their bodies and brains did come from me; so somewhere inside I must have been a carrier. The security and confidence they have must be, at least in part, because you have helped me give it to them. God, if I had a choice of hoarding my talent and my mind and soul, using it for my own gratification, or passing it on to others, my children, my friends, and those I could help, naturally I would not choose any different way than the road I have taken. It would be against my nature, against *all* nature.

God, help me to be grateful that I can be a vessel.

JAYNE

❧

"This precious treasure—this light and power that now shine within us—is held in a perishable container, that is, in our weak bodies. Everyone can see that the glorious power within must be from God and is not our own" (2 Cor. 4:7).

And the People
with No Humility

God:

I get so sick of people who are always and invariably *right*. It seems that no one but me ever makes a mistake. My husband is so right about everything that it's disgusting. (Sometimes, Father, I think I could forgive him for anything except always being right!)

He's not the only one either, God. I wanted to develop self-confidence in our children. I figure it takes assurance to visualize any ability or success, and it has seemed to me that without visualizing it, it is impossible to put into effect. So I have encouraged and admired and tried literally to follow the biblical advice, "If there be anything worthy of good report, if there be any virtue, if there be any praise . . ." But, Father, I think I've overdone it!

Some of my friends also seem intent upon displaying their superior abilities and opinions and accomplishments. Their lack of humility makes me feel more humble than ever. Too humble! It seems that they all feed their ego off mine. The more they get, the less I have. (I wish they'd all get indigestion.)

Yet, Father, help me to remember that when people brag about themselves they are actually crying out for help and they can't put it into the right words. Help me to reinterpret their actions in order to supply the words. After all, no one talks about himself if he feels someone else will do it for him or if he is already sure of himself.

Father, I have asked to be your vessel, to see beneath the "false garments" and superficial disguises of those I love. Help me to know when they are reaching to me for help, and help me recognize the inner person inside each and give him the help he needs.

JAYNE

❧

"God gives strength to the humble, but sets himself against the proud and haughty" (James 4:6).

Lord,
Please Make My Relationships
with Other People Real

Father:

I beg you, please help me empty myself of these recurrent feelings of being disconnected and somehow displaced, of having to be conscious of myself and needing to compete in the world. Why should I feel that other people are compelling me to compete? You never meant people to compete with each other. You made each person special and different.

What makes me feel locked up and left out—"different"—when the earthly scores are counted? Lord, what makes me feel uncomfortable and threatened? Why can't I meet other humans on their level?

There are probably lots of people who feel like me. Why is it that I must feel superior or else my sense of ego-centeredness makes me feel inferior? It's as if every other person intimidates me, as though everything must be relative to my own ego.

How often I've had to fight these impulses to such soulless attitudes! Father, I feel superior and better than some people sometimes. (How can this person be so dense and so stupid?) And at other times I feel so inadequate that something compels me to put on airs and try to make the other person feel less, by comparison, so I can be more. ("My husband and I just returned from a frightfully expensive tour, but it was so exciting!")

God, I'm sorry when I have such spiritually traitorous attitudes and do such wretched things. I want to meet every other person without superficial attitudes and this dreadfully heavy mask of ego. I want to realize my part in others and theirs in me without these armors of disguise and self-delusion that prevent us from ever really knowing one another.

I know that before I can ever do this I have to get above this drive that somehow causes me to plant little ideas of status into my talk. Even the tiniest type of bragging ruins everything. I have to have no pretenses. I can't have earthly arrogance if I'm to have the remotest chance of penetrating other people where they live their inner life. I can't be false at all. Especially my humbleness can't be false.

Also I must completely thrust off the insecurity that makes me apologize foolishly or be self-effacing. This is also conceit. It's actually a bid for reassurance, a symptom of too much self-concern and self-love.

In fact, I can't have any thought of myself at all. If I must be conscious of myself as an ego, I know it must be simply: This is me. The *real* me. Take it or leave it, but I have something I want to give you. I trust us both to God who makes us what we are. No props— just you, just me, making "us."

Please, God, help this small vessel of you, that is me, to be larger.

LUCY

❧

"Don't grumble about each other, brothers" (James 5:9).

I Am Afraid of Competition

Dear God:

I'm fed up with thinking of myself as inferior. It's terrible to feel intimidated by competition, and, God, I have no confidence that I can do things well. Under pressure I freeze. My friends act as if it's so important to win in everything that I'm defeated before I start. I don't even put up a fight when people want to beat me.

Jody and Jan and lots of the other girls play bridge so much that I couldn't keep up even if I did have the knack for cards and figuring numbers. I'm not challenged when I finally get a "hand." Not me! I'm horrified! Yet, God, I want to play because if I don't I won't get invited and I won't have these friends. But how I long to have the game over.

I want to play golf, but I hate to hit the ball, and that's what it's all about. I'm afraid to try to hit the ball because if I don't hit it well I'll make a disgraceful score and have to turn it in. (Sometimes I wish I could tell a little white lie like some girls do, but I can't even do a good job of that!)

I'm a great joy to my friends. They can always count on my inferiority and feel more important themselves. I haven't got the guts to change, even if I wanted to deprive them of their pleasure. In a way, I don't think I even want to. I probably enjoy the added popularity of being inferior.

I'm sure I could play the piano well enough to let other people hear me, but no one even knows I can play. This inner defeat mechanism makes me feel everyone would wait to hear me make mistakes. Then, thinking I'm going to hit the wrong notes, I'm sure to do it.

But, God, it's a form of conceit to think it's of any great importance to anyone else what I do or don't do. Sure, they would all like to beat me and feel important in comparison. If I just lie down and let them do it, they'll walk on me. But I'm not going to let them anymore. If they want to, it's just their tough luck! I'm not going to feel done in by the idea of competing with them. After all, Father, I'm not competing with anyone but myself for my best actions—for you. If I don't take care of me and do my best, no one is going to do it for me, not even you.

God, I don't think I'm going to make any more complaints to you about my complexes and hang-ups. I'm sick to death of them, and I'm going to disregard them.

It's an insult to you that I still carry over insecurities from childhood. Now that I know you and belong to you, I know that you work through me. Therefore, I am invulnerable, capable, and poised, and there is nothing I can't cope with.

God, I have held the wrong mental picture of myself

for so long that even without realizing it I have brought it on myself. The spiritual law is that we must visualize *who* we are and anything that we want to be or do *before* it can become a reality. So I know what I am going to do and what I am not going to do! I'm *not* going to think of myself anymore as a loser (even in social ways). It's really ridiculous, God, when, through you, I have so much more going for me than most people.

If my feeling of inadequacy is a subconscious generosity for others' feelings, I'm sorry, God, but my unselfishness just doesn't stretch that far anymore. Especially when feeding off my ego doesn't really do anyone any good anyway.

From now on I'm going to visualize myself as a winner! I'm as smart as anyone. My accomplishments can prove it. I'm not going to be a chameleon to other people's vibrations. I refuse to be so susceptible to others' competitiveness that I can't play their games.

If life has to be full of big and little competitions, I think you want me to get in there and do "my thing" as well or better than anyone. Inside I know I can. God, you can make it possible for me to keep an image of myself in my inner eye that you have of me.

Help me to know who I am. Help me to realize your strength in me.

JAYNE

✦

"Friendly suggestions are as pleasant as perfume" (*Prov.* 27:9).

I Want to Be Well Liked

Dear God:

You know it's not like I had a legion of friends. I don't have too many. So yesterday when my friend ignored me, I was utterly hurt. I swear, God, it wasn't my imagination. She really gave me the "cold" treatment. I was at Annie's coffee, and there was someone new there, an impressive career girl from New York. But was that a reason for Polly deliberately to look the other way when I tried to talk to her and wanted to join the conversation?

God, I wonder. Do you suppose Polly is somehow ashamed of me? Does she think I don't measure up when she wants to make a special impression? Or, God, could it be just plain jealousy and possessiveness with Polly?

Something even worse occurs to me when Polly does this, and you know, God, this isn't the first time she's done it. I feel so exposed to Polly. I see now that I never should have put myself in that position. I never should have confided in her as I have. She knows me clear through and through, and when she shows disapproval, it's different from someone doing it who doesn't know me. You know what I mean.

I wonder about friendship. What is it anyway? I don't think that Polly very often (if ever) thinks about me as a person. I guess she really couldn't care less. With Polly, what matters is what I think of *her.* How do I make her think about *herself?* Does she feel secure and good with me? If so, she likes me. When she doesn't, then she doesn't like me.

But who am I to criticize? I guess I'm pretty much the same way. They say that the traits we are most likely to dislike in someone else are most often the very ones we have ourselves. The times I like Polly the least are when she makes me feel insecure. Though it sounds conceited, maybe my presence around the special guest at the party made Polly feel inadequate.

Really it's an awful thing, a cynical thing, a hateful thing, to come up with the idea that we are so insecure that our so-called affections are based on nothing more than mutual aid in self-imagery. I guess all our hangups go back to the awful separation, the sentences that we seem to have to serve before we can get back home to you, no matter how we beg for probation.

I sometimes feel so isolated, God.

How can we (Polly and I) learn that there is nothing to fear from each other, that we need each other? How, God, can we know that we must lose ourselves in order to find ourselves?

I know who I am because God is in me, Christ lives in me. Inside, where I really am, I am capable, poised, and sufficient. There are no answers that don't already live within me. Your Holy Spirit is my central core.

There need be no struggle to reach beyond myself or outside of myself. It's just *there*—the real me (and the real Polly)—dependable, undeniable, available. This is true because inside me and all about me and around all of us you are always there.

Help me, God, and help Polly, too, to understand *who* we are.

BARB

❧

"There are 'friends' who pretend to be friends, but there is a friend who sticks closer than a brother" (Prov. 18:24).

FORGIVE US OUR TRESPASSES

Wanting Another Man

Dear God:

Emmett went out of town, and Bob showed up. He told me he'd always had a "special feeling" for me, and he tried to take me in his arms.

Fran and Bob had had a fight, and Fran had made Bob feel rejected. He needed a friend, not a lover! But when I heard the words, "I love you," I turned to butter.

Oh, God, I was scared—not of Bob, but of me. Bob and Fran have been friends with Emmett and me for years. Bob surely doesn't love me like Emmett does, but Emmett doesn't say he does! A man's heart may be in his stomach, but a woman's heart is surely in her ears.

How I quivered inside! I yearned with a longing I would have been hard put to control for another minute when Jan came in, bringing the tap shoes Becky left at her house. Thank you, God, for protecting me with this interruption. I ask the strength that you have promised through claiming me as your child that this won't ever happen to me again.

Yet I know temptation is part of life, and through withstanding temptation we get stronger and become worthy of you. The Bible is full of accounts of men and women tempted this way because love can never be deep and real without being proved. So you have allowed us free will and have allowed us to go through these unchristlike yearnings. If I had no choice except to love you, my love could never be worthy of you.

Marty and I were discussing why you allowed evil in our world. She said, if there were only one man and one woman in the world, there could be love, but how much more perfect a love if there were another man. Making a choice between the two would strengthen that love and make it real and strong. Because we have made our choice to be with you, it means much more.

To give into a temptation such as I experienced is not my choice. It is not what I really want, no matter how such images of forbidden fruits grab at my imagination. I know my body is your temple.

In dying, Christ actually made his strength available to me. His power went into each disciple. If I put my trust in you, it is not possible for me to be tempted beyond my ability to withstand or to be forced to act as though your strength were not in me.

As for growing older (and my female desire to feel still desirable as a female), I know you have a plan for each age. Like Paul, I want to ask that in whatever state I'm in I be content.

God, I know you have made love and sex to be part of the same. The sex act is an outer means of expressing deepest inner devotion to another person. Sex cheaply given has to cheapen love.

JANET

❧

"We need have no fear of someone who loves us perfectly; his perfect love for us eliminates all dread of what he might do to us. If we are afraid, it is for fear of what he might do to us, and shows that we are not fully convinced that he really loves us" (1 John 4:18).

Embarrassed for Him

Dear God:

I feel more adequate than my husband. I don't want to put him down because, really, he is sweet in ways that no one but me could know or appreciate, but being sweet doesn't make it. I'm embarrassed that he says the dumb things that people kind of snicker over and cover up, or change the subject. I try to signal him, but he doesn't catch on. Poor darling, I know so well how he feels because I feel it for him. Yet I wish he could be like Dot's husband, debonair, always up to every social or business situation, not needing anyone's indulgence or understanding, not having to endure anyone's superiority. If only there was some way to invent a remote control for a husband.

Worse still, O God, forgive me for being human, but I think I'm smarter than he is sometimes. The truth is, I feel for me. People judge me by him. They judge us as one unit, and sometimes I think this just isn't my dish.

Make me brave and big enough to cover this so he never knows. God, it would kill him if he knew.

God, I don't want to be ungrateful and look to outside material things. No one but me knows him like I do; so they're not in a position to judge him. Help me to remember the special individual he is in your eyes—and in mine! Let me remember that he has taken me as his lifelong commitment and done the very best he could.

God, women are somewhat spoiled in a way, and I don't want to be a spoiled woman looking to what I'm getting all the time rather than what I can give and what I can appreciate. That isn't the real me because it can't be your will.

Women aren't always as grateful as they should be to their mates. When we marry, our husbands take responsibility for all our needs. My husband has furnished my needs all these years—the clothes I have worn, the bills I have run up for health, food, and home. He's worked every day, all day, to do it, and he has taken good care of the children. Our family has been his whole reason for everything. To care for me has been his life. Help me appreciate him like I should, even when it's hard.

Maybe, God, if I see him in a clearer light and picture him in my own mind as the person I know he is, and the special person you and I both know he is inside, I might find the world would see him differently, too.

EVELYN

93

❧

"For a husband is in charge of his wife in the same way Christ is in charge of his body the church. (He gave his very life to take care of it and be its Savior!)" (Eph. 5:23).

May I Forget Myself
and Think of Others

God:

You're all-powerful, and more than anything I want
to be your instrument. So please help me try to do better about interpreting and guessing and reinterpreting
the needs of others. Help me see inside other people
even when they seem antagonistic.

Father, help me to love extra when people in my life
seem most unlovable. This is really when they need
your love (through mine) the most. So, immediately,
before I become too upset, I want to offer up some special things to your will. Where I am weak, I can be
strong through you.

Sometimes my children's attitudes really hurt. They
seem not to care about me, and I wonder if they'll ever
become responsible. For example, the other day I asked
Jeff to mow the yard. He said, "It's too hot. If it's cooler
when I get back from playing tennis, I'll do it then."
(He played tennis, and I mowed the yard.)

Particularly I want to remember and be able to offer
to you the hurt I sometimes feel when John seems so

rigid and aloof that I can't help but wonder if he's still in love with me. I also want to offer up the times when he nags and when he's irritable and short-tempered. Sometimes he makes me feel left out; I can't seem to reach him, and he doesn't let me feel like a part of his life, his triumphs, or even his sorrows. These times so disappoint me and give me such an impotent feeling of resentment that I may act foolishly, and I'm sorry later. When I feel he is rejecting me, I often say cutting and belittling things to him. I behave like a child wanting to strike out and get even.

Father, it sure seems a not-very-funny twist to home life that it's often easier to deal constructively with someone else's children or husband than with my own. I guess it's because I'm too emotionally involved with my own. And by emotionally involved, what I really mean is that I'm too much involved with my own ego and self-image. I should know better than to say and do some things. God, you've made me smarter than I sometimes act.

I can cope with others through your love. Gentle reactions are far better than "coming-on-strong" and stirring up a fight. "Coming-on-soft" makes other people turn softer too, and you've told me to deal with other people like I want them to treat me. That means I must mentally step into their shoes and think how they feel (in their secret places), how it seems to them, before I allow myself to get boxed in by my own personality in a shell of self-isolation.

Anyway, I'm thankful, Father, that your love has made it so much easier for me to be objective about other people. You've made it possible for me not to care too much what happens to me in outside circumstances because I love you more than myself.

JAYNE

"This explains why a man leaves his father and mother and is joined to his wife in such a way that the two become one person" (Gen. 2:24).

AS WE FORGIVE THOSE
WHO TRESPASS AGAINST US

The Awful Fight

Dear God:

Last night Howard and I engaged in that wonderful outlet you provide for in marriage—verbal warfare! Howard slept like a baby afterwards, and I hardly got a wink. Now, God, I have a headache. Is this the reward I get for all the brilliant strategy—the clever, cutting words said and unsaid?

Howard went blissfully off to dreamland as I was just sharpening my tongue and mind to the proper pitch for the occasion. Since he no longer heard me, I should have talked to you and it would have all been over, but I didn't want to, at least not until I wallowed in the snug blanket of self-righteousness. The whole thing got clear out of control! I'm the one who was right (I just know I was); yet I'm the one who got burned.

The rest of the night and all day long I've thought of more and more ways I could have won a point or two, or put it better and accused him of more. But now I have no way to get even, no way to get it out.

I always think there is some way to win. I haven't yet! And I remember how it took hours (off and on) even to get a good fight started!

I have to pray now, God. He'll be home soon, and even if I'm right, I can't stand another round.

Dear Lord, help me not to repeat the things I said. As a child of yours you would not have put me in a family situation I couldn't cope with. I love Howard. Howard loves me. He will always take care of me, and he also seeks to do your will.

Thank you for sending the Great Mediator.

SUE

✤

"So if you are standing before the altar in the Temple, offering a sacrifice to God, and suddenly remember that a friend has something against you, leave your sacrifice there beside the altar and go and apologize and be reconciled to him, and then come and offer your sacrifice to God" (Matt. 5:23–24).

Oh God! He Flirts!

Dear God:

Every time we go to a party, everyone makes over Brad! He's gotten better looking, Father, and I have gotten worse. Let's face it. He aged better than I, and though he started out ahead of me, it seems that now people will ask him, any day, if I am his mother! Oh, God, I couldn't stand that. Has any other woman in all of history had such a terrible problem?

Besides that, Brad must be going through a "stage" (a worse stage than usual) because he seems to mentally size-up the vital statistics and fantasize over every beautiful young girl he can feast his eyes on. And *flirt!* Oh, God, at parties he makes passes. He flirts outrageously—and with my best friends! He even asks them for a soirée on the tennis courts at midnight. Imagine! Or to meet him on the ninth hole! Of course, we all know he's kidding, but no one knows, God, how I resent this.

God, sometimes I'm afraid. I don't feel adequate. Help me know what I can do. You have said that if we ask, you will be right here. You are our loving and always present Father, ready to help and to answer us. When we knock, you will open and in no way cast us out. If I ask you a question—even an earthly, everyday type question such as I know thousands of other women must also ask—"How can I be sure of holding my husband?" you will answer me. All I need do is listen inside and be ready to receive your answer.

You have said that whatever you take away from us you always send something better. Maybe this time of trial will turn out to be a problem that makes me stronger. Maybe if I try harder, I can make him happier with me, and stronger too. Send me the Holy Spirit, Father, because you have the power to make me adequate and invulnerable.

God, I don't know the answers. I don't know what will cause this nightmare to go away, but that's still all right because you know all about it. Whatever your will for me is, it is also my will. Help me to recognize the help in your closeness and constant connection with me.

I only ask, God, that each day, and with each hang-up or problem or challenge, I might see your direction and do as you would have me do.

SHANNON

❧

*"And why quibble about the speck in someone else's eye
—his little fault—when a board is in your own? . . . Hyp-
ocrite! First get rid of the board, and then perhaps you
can see well enough to deal with his speck!"* (Luke 6:41–
42).

When He Doesn't Want Sex

Dear God:

Again when it was time to go to bed last night, he said he had a terrible headache. Oh, my heart almost broke. I thought surely tonight, after he had been gone and it has been so long, he would want me. The truth is, God, for some reason he doesn't want me at all anymore. And I have to be calm. I have to think. What could the reason be? Am I so undesirable? Another woman? A feeling of impotency on his part? (Maybe that time I was impatient, scornful—could that be it?) Is he afraid of his own potency? Afraid to be exposed? Or is he just plain too tired?

Even if the worst is true, I know that you have told us that we get more from giving than getting, and this isn't pure selflessness. It's really true. If he doesn't love, he is the loser—not me. God, I remember that when I was young others loved me but I got nothing out of it because I didn't love them. It gave me no pleasure at all. It has given me great joy to love my husband, not to be loved, but to *love*.

Help me to remember that perfect love casts out fear. If he is afraid of being inadequate, if I love him enough, he could have no fear with me. God, help me to love him with your love, a pure love that is empty of all selfishness. Make my love worthy as your love for us is always worthy. God, erase the selfish, ego-ridden, proud woman inside of me and let the real person that you have made me come through. Help me to let him know how much I love him. Help me to let him know that it's not only his body or his virility I love but that I love him for the person he is—the real eternal him. Help me to make him feel important so that he will know that nothing could ever happen to make me not satisfied with him or feel that he is inadequate in any way.

Help him, God, to see himself through my eyes. And, God, if it isn't true (if sometimes it's difficult to feel the way I must act), may we keep it just our secret— between you and me.

JOANN

❧

"The one who obeys me is the one who loves me; and because he loves me, my Father will love him; and I will too, and I will reveal myself to him" (John 14:21).

God,
Could He Be Unfaithful?

Dear God:

My husband seems to lead a separate life entirely. Business I understand. Social sometimes. But how "separate" is reasonable? Maybe even another woman?

What does my husband do on these frequent business trips, all to the same place? He's always excited when he's going. I can tell; he doesn't even sleep he is so keyed up with anticipation. What have I done, God? Why could he be so eager to get away from me? Or is there another reason?

Shall I check up on him? Hire a private detective? God, do I really want to know? What am I to do after I find out? I am no longer young (firm, sexy, appealing). I know this. But maybe just to know one way or another. Could this be some twenty-two-year-old chick?

Suppose it is true. I've repeatedly dieted, but oh, God, I just can't get off that extra ten pounds. As soon as I do, the kids go on an eating jag, and I have to cook and *I have* to eat. I just can't help it. I don't know what to do.

Can I share him? With this awful knife-cutting hurt? This sense of inadequacy and worthlessness? And this insecurity every time he leaves? Yet how can I stop him? To check up on him might force the issue and bring the whole thing to a head, and he would leave me!

I need him, God. I need a father for my children; I need to be supported while I raise them, no matter how my private heart aches. There is still Mary's dancing recital, Bill's "Group" and Bluebirds for Sharon, and Sunday school to teach for Scott.

And, oh, God, maybe I'm wrong to feel this way about pride. Pride should be way down the line, but I just can't bear to have my friends know and say, "Poor dear! How could he treat her like that?"

But, God, you would not have put me here with this man and in this home unless this is the place you meant me to be. I would not be here with these problems if these were not the very troubles that would teach me the lessons I must learn in order to advance.

I am needed here. If I were not needed, I wouldn't be here. If there were some other man, some other home, a place where I could feel more cherished and cared for, you would have put me there unless there is some real reason why I can do more good here.

My husband needs me. He has his own problems and cares and unhappiness. He needs my loyalty in any event. If he is going through a stage or rough waters, he needs my support and all the understanding I can muster because he can't possibly be happy himself when he is doing wrong.

Help me, Father, to remember and appreciate all the good times, the good things we have shared, the life that we have welded together.

You have brought me this far safely. You will be with me the rest of the journey. I have only to trust in you.

MARTHA

❧

"Your heavenly Father will forgive you if you forgive those who sin against you; but if you refuse to forgive them, he will not forgive you" (Matt. 6:14–15).

LEAD US NOT INTO TEMPTATION

Worry over Money

Dear God:

I'm afraid we won't have enough money. We live too much on credit. Suppose we can't pay our bills? What if we can't supply the needs of the kids? What if someone got terribly sick? I'm afraid.

But how can I be afraid? Tired, maybe, but never can I for one moment consider *anything* too much. Father, you are all-powerful. Your strength is mine, and I am your instrument. This conviction goes so much deeper and is more important than any exterior problems and fears, or bills. This is my *true home*. This is where all our bills are paid even before they come due.

How can I turn loose the fearful side of my mind? How can I let go? In good times I even distrust too much joy because I haven't earned it. At the moment when I have no problems, I'm not able to feel comfortable in security.

God, my trouble is, I don't trust it (or you) to last, and I am so ashamed of this. If I ever felt guilty about anything, it's this! How could I not trust you when you so obviously have chosen me and done all these extraordinary things for me? All my wants have always been met by you.

I have based my life on my faith in you. Still, I am afraid to let go completely. My earth-boundness keeps pulling me back each time I start to soar, and I have not yet freed myself from the devil's hold.

I wanted so much to buy a new dress for the party my club had this spring. I was almost frantic worrying about it, and I knew we couldn't afford it. I can't imagine now, God, how I could have bothered you about such a thing. After all, Eve got by with nothing but a fig leaf! I'd gladly settle for a "fig leaf" if it'd help me avoid the temptation with the "apple."

But I will endure! I no longer take anything so seriously, only you and your all-powerfulness, your plan! You always provide for your children.

Nothing can long stand against this—no fear against this joy, no confusion against this purpose. Only as long as it serves your purpose can anything touch your children. I must completely trust and completely empty myself of self-consciousness, willfulness, and self-directiveness before you, Father, can truly use me or even help me.

I must be only yours—entirely yours. Then I can't worry.

And incidentally, God, I am sorry I worried so about money. I know you say to waste no thought—beyond constructive self-help—on how you will meet our material needs. Our bills are also yours. You know what we need. You will take care of our needs in the best way at the best time. You are worthy of all our love and trust. Please forgive me.

Sue

❧

"God cares so wonderfully for flowers that are here today and gone tomorrow, won't he more surely care for you, O men of little faith?" (Matt. 6:30).

Going to the Dentist

Dear God:

Well, this is the morning marked on my calendar with a big red exclamation point. I go to the dentist! No matter how I've been telling myself that it's stupid to get hung up on the small things, I still do it. It isn't a small thing to me.

Right now I can see in my mind the whole gruesome scene: the smiling, jovial dentist looking like a lurking Dr. Jekyll in a satanic mask; my legs quaking and my teeth chattering as I try to return his happy forced chitchat. Behind his back he's holding that awful contraption (that I've never looked at) and is trying to relax "the patient's nerves" (as he was told to do in dental school). All this inevitably leads to the time he clanks the cold steel thing in my mouth! It seems like hours that he weaves the needle around in my gums. The Novocaine shot is every bit as bad as the pain of the drill could be. The drill buzzes like bees on my nerves while I wait dead-faced and bone-tense for the bite and sting of his jabs burrowing into spots where his deadening process didn't work.

Now look, God, this is ridiculous! Why can't a person tolerate the small pains that a doctor inflicts? After all, I wouldn't blow my cool over the little aches and pains of daily life. I hardly notice them, and his tortures are no worse.

I feel kind of sorry for these poor guys, the doctors. So many people dread their "ministrations of mercy." Well, God, as far as I'm concerned I'm nothing but a gutless coward. I ought to be ashamed! I am!

After all, you are in me. If I remember who I am and to whom I belong, I'll see that the person I'm acting like and feeling like right now doesn't resemble the *real me* at all. Now you just have to help me remember because without your help, I can barely manage to face this dentist, let alone the *big things!*

But you are immovable, invulnerable, always stable, and able to cope with anything. If I share your strength, I'm all these things too (like poised and assured and calm). So, God, I'm asking you to help me, and I'm claiming your strength and courage for *all* the little and the big things.

After all, I *can* claim you. I'm yours! So, I'm turning myself over to you. You start with the outside of me (my quivers and shakes) and work into the inner core of calm that is going to be the real me (at the dentist and always).

Now I see it's time to go, and I'm quite ready for it. For heaven's sake! Now that I remember how close you are to me, Lord, and how I belong to you, I really can't imagine how I was filled with such dread of a kindly, innocuous dentist!

Well, doctor! Here I come! And I'm going to meet you (and everything and everybody else, too) head on—beginning now.

Thank you, God.

JAYNE

❧

"If I go up to heaven, you are there; if I go down to the place of the dead, you are there" (Ps. 139:8).

Presiding at Club

Dear God:

Let me tell you something, God. I have to preside over the Tuesday afternoon ritual at our Tuesday Afternoon Club. About thirty-five of my friends will be there, and I am going to faint. I am going to be the first woman ever to faint and have to be carried out from such an occasion. Or maybe I'll be sick and vomit right there. Or worse still, maybe I'll make a Freudian slip. Maybe I'll say *intercourse* when I mean *introduce*. "Now it is my great pleasure, ladies, to *intercourse* Mr. Smith!" Oh, the snickers, the dead silence, the uproarious laughter, the silent disapproval, the embarrassment. Now that I think of it, I know it is impossible to open my mouth without the word *intercourse* going through my mind so strongly every single minute that I will not be able to enunciate another word. When I open my mouth to say anything else, that is the word that is sure to come out. I'm going to be sick right now, God, just thinking about it!

No such absolute gutless coward has ever before

lived in history. Tell me, God, whatever am I to do about me?

I have to preside, but I've built up a big thing about it, and I'm terribly afraid. No one else seems to suffer this way. I watch others, holding papers, get up and report. The paper doesn't even quiver! But when I get up, the crinkling and crackling of my notes can be heard and seen clear across the room.

Young girls and boys on TV (with millions of people watching) carry on without a falter, seemingly without a quiver. Suppose they forgot the lyrics or the lines? Suppose they got sick right there and had to be carried off? Suppose they fainted or disgraced themselves? Yet in all the hours I have watched TV and all that I've ever heard of, I have never known of such an occurrence.

God, I can always tell you anything in prayer and you will understand. Prayer is a dialogue, not a monologue. It's a partnership, both ways, between you and me. I mustn't simply pour out my fears and hang-ups, but I must listen. When I listen to you, you really are talking to me and what you are telling me is that I really can trust you completely. You will never let anything that is not of your will happen to me. You would not will me to suffer the things I fear. I can be safe with you. When I seek guidance, I can't get anything at all, but when I seek you, I get guidance, and then I have everything.

Nothing more is needed. I am unafraid. I leave all my silly little worries with you, knowing nothing can ever happen outside of your will. You are in me; so I

know I am capable and confident and poised and able
to stand stable, unaffected by any fear or circumstance.

JAYNE

❧

*"Now go ahead and do as I tell you, for I will help you
to speak well, and I will tell you what to say" (Exod. 4:12).*

BUT DELIVER US FROM EVIL

My Mother's
In The Hospital

Dear God:

My mother is in the hospital. She's suffering. Even now, as I sit here writing, she is crying out in pain.

This morning I got out of bed and smiled at the new day. I forgot for a while. I sang as I cooked the family breakfast.

She woke up to face moment-to-moment stabbing hurts which would stretch into interminable hours of private hell this day—a test of her endurance that she could scarcely pass.

I feel fine. Nothing hurts me. Pain seems so far from me in my health that I can hardly remember what it's like. For mother, everything hurts.

And I remember about her now, and I feel my heart crack. How can the day sing on as though nothing were dislocated, all patches of sunshine, while even now there are those holding on to a searing lifeline of despair beyond the reach of light?

Oh, God, how I wish I could somehow take away their agonies. Oh, Father, I am ashamed now for feeling joy in myself. It feels all wrong for people to be lapping up pleasure when others are troubled and heavy laden. I can't possibly sail glibly and blithely on when my mother or brother or sister or child has found life so difficult.

It is somehow uncomfortable and unbalanced, the happiness and bursting joy, the sadness and sorrow, all at the same time. For me to take all the joy seems selfish and unfeeling.

There are some things I definitely do not want to happen to my brothers or sisters. I don't want such experiences for them or for myself. My instinctive reaction to the fear I feel for them (or for me) is to fight back mentally and emotionally with all that's in me. Like a prisoner in chains, I kick and scream impotently against the unavoidable. I am still your rebellious willful child.

If I could drain off my joy, siphon it out of me, I would project it onto those in despair. I would use the unwoven cloth of it to spin a protective armor about them.

God, it's not that I want them taken out of the world. I don't believe that is the answer. My life has proven that to be in the world, with the God-armor encasing me, can be to have all the advantages of being where the action is. At the same time, it can mean having all the wonder and awe of being where the peace is. Nothing can actually be too much, and nothing can pierce the pressurized compartment where I live.

I think I'm forgetting your plan. All of us should suffer to refine our souls. The suffering is really a small and unimportant part when seen from your all-encompassing point of view. Even while we are passing through it, we are in reality quite safe in your grasp.

But we must all suffer the illusion, too, of suffering alone. No one can do it for us, and we can't do it for anyone else. Much as we'd like to go with our dear ones (or everyone) in the valley of the shadow when their times come, we can't fit the slot, and they must go on alone. No one gains through unproductive and unconstructive vicarious suffering. It only weakens us for the time to come when we each will need all our conserved strength for our own mission. Jesus seems to be the only one who has really mastered the ability to use vicarious suffering for helping others, except in the prayer sense.

And who am I to argue with your will? How can I know what is best when you have all-encompassing sight and know everything?

So now, it is your will that my mother suffer. You are all-powerful. I base my life on this belief. You are able to keep that which is committed unto you. Nothing can possibly happen that is outside your will. Whether or not I can visualize safety for her, you are still with my mother as surely as you are everywhere. She is in the safe circle of your arms, and your presence fills her hospital room. And you are still with me as you always are.

God, help me to remember. I would not stand between her and your will even if I could. I'm always your servant. I'll not resist. Your grace is sufficient for all of us. Giving ourselves up to your will is our peace.

JAYNE

✿

"He will wipe away all tears from their eyes, and there shall be no more death, nor sorrow, nor crying, nor pain. All of that has gone forever" (Rev. 21:4).

The Death Wish

Dear God:

I'm scared. I've heard that death is a subconscious wish. Even though I don't consciously want to die, I think I have that wish. When a woman's primary job is completed, she feels she isn't needed and that there isn't much reason to go on living.

I suppose men feel this way too. They say this is why so many men have heart attacks at this age. Cancer and "accidents" that happen in middle life are often a "death wish" more than an accident. This scares me, God, because the children are all independent now and our home-nest is empty. John has reached the height of his job, and everything he does seems to be motivated by "business." God, instead of feeling proud and happy for him, I am often jealous and resentful and feel more inadequate than ever because he is so adequate. I'm too young and alive to be put to the permanent post-child-care pasture. Maybe secretly I'm opting for some of the ideas of the Women's Liberation Movement. I don't want a man's responsibilities, but I would like some of his importance and place in the world.

Oh, God, I hate the idea of going down that sad, well-worn path so many middle-aged and older women have trod—the women's clubs, playing bridge and golf, the partying, and the attempts at "fun." This process of anesthetizing the senses doesn't seem to help with the years of widowhood, the aloneness and fears and illnesses of the retirement home, and worst of all, being a burdensome duty to the children!

There seems to be nothing left that is useful for me to do now but housework. And, God, I am *so sick* of ordinary jobs. Will I never get to the end of them? *No!* What a silly question. Of course I won't! It goes on and on: cleaning johns, scooping up dust and dirt of everyone from the accidents of the animals to the messy thoughtlessness of my husband. Garbage and refuse! And no end to it! Am I wrong, God, sometimes to think I might have been made for higher things?

Even while I think these thoughts, I feel ashamed, God. Surely a real woman could content herself to live through and for her man and could do all the little extra things I don't do (like I wish I would) in order to make him feel secure. I should do these things even though they do sometimes seem just a fringe concern in his life. Help me, God, to grasp fulfillment from my belief that behind every successful man there needs to be a woman playing a supportive role.

When I think of the "death wish," I realize that I have no business letting my mind even wander over ideas that are foreign to my beliefs. You have given me this life, and you'll take it when you're ready. As long as you leave me here, there has to be a reason in your overall plan. I'm committed to my work here in the home even when I wish you had higher expectations for me. Life goes on and on, and the only constant thing in this life is renewal and change.

Nothing that is done, no effort that is made, is ever truly lost, and no one we have ever loved can be lost because we, too, are being constantly reborn.

JAYNE

"With all the earnestness I have I tell you this—no one who obeys me shall ever die" (John 8:51).

When a Friend
Is Dying of Cancer

Dear God:

A close friend is dying of cancer. She is so brave, so beautiful, so grounded in faith, and so *alive* that when I look at her I can't possibly imagine that in a few short months she will be gone. Gone—where? Gone as though she never had breathed and loved and shared and smiled and filled a place in this world.

Is this true of all of us? We are so *alive* today that we can scarcely imagine how we could live if not in this world (or how the world could possibly go on without us); yet we will be called to face our own death. And the persons we are today will be the same inner persons who are called upon to die!

And not only that. But the same Jayne Bremyer I am at this moment will someday stand by and see loved ones die—slip away from my frantic grasp—and become inanimate shells. That my life could ever hold such an experience seems inconceivable. These things happen to other people, not me. I am *here* and *real*, and my husband John is *here* and *real*. It is impossible that he could ever be no more than the rustle of wings down dim caverns of my memory.

Can I really face this kind of intellectual knowledge that I can't imagine emotionally? You have said that though we take the wings of the morning and dwell in the uttermost parts of the sea, even there your hand will lead us and your right hand will hold us.

Lucy believes you will always be there. She is sure you will be with her in trouble as you have been with her every day. She knows that you have guided her this far and that you will be with her yet.

Help me to know that sufficient for the day is the trouble thereof—but not yesterday or tomorrow. Only today is mine. You will be with me tomorrow as surely as you are here today.

God, another friend is a nurse. She says that when humans reach the final departure point and face death, each person has a special fund of strength from which to draw. She says it seems never to fail. It's true; you are always there.

Help me to realize, God, that as long as I live with you there's nothing to fear. I will always be with you, and I will always live!

JAYNE

&

"He will remove the cloud of gloom, the pall of death that hangs over the earth; he will swallow up death forever" (Isa. 25:7–8).

133

For the Loved Ones
Left Behind

Dear God:

I have no fear of dying or the pain and suffering accompanying dying or death itself. Many times I long for the glorious release from struggles put upon the physical life.

My fear is not of *death* but of *separation*—separation from my family, my separation from them and their separation from me. Would I look down upon them or walk beside them longing to share their cares? Would I feel, "If only I could help?" Would I be so far removed as never to consider them again, or remember, or what?

Where is my faith in "Eye hath not seen nor ear heard, neither have entered into the heart of man, the things God hath prepared for them that love him"? I'm trying to rationalize humanly what would logically be.

Lord, help me to know you are not bound by my mind. If I am incapable of imagining "forever," how could I possibly imagine the filling of that time?

134

Free me of my fear of separation from my family. On the other hand, dear Lord, how would they weather separation from me?

It would put a terrific financial strain on Howard. He would have to hire a sitter for Neil. There are many financial shortcuts I take in my household money management he isn't aware of. He doesn't understand grocery sales and fresh fruit and prepackaged foods or good clothing buys. He can't sew! He'd have to marry again, and that's all right. But would he be careful?

Lord, I'm not giving him credit! I'm telling you what he should do. Please, Lord, you tell him what to do if this occasion ever arises. You be his guide.

But, if I should leave, who will teach Darla to be a proper lady? She would have a lot of responsibility for such a young age. And Neil would never know the mother who gave him birth and taught him to pat-a-cake! Dan wouldn't have his short mom to pat on the head and say, "Now, mom, don't lose your cool," when he knew he deserved a good spanking.

These concerns of mine come from you, Lord. You gave mothers a special place that requires a sense of others' needs. Without a feeling of importance and self-confidence that we can do the job best, we would fail.

But still, God, I need to have more humility. Help me to understand, deep down in my heart where such fears are, that I will be kept in this family circle as long as I am needed. You won't remove me if you haven't prepared a way for Darla to become what you plan for her to be. If my leaving is emotionally and financially difficult for Howard, you still have a plan to take care of this or a reason for it to be.

Dear Lord, I pray then for your will to be done in this family. Help me prepare to let go, as I inevitably must do.

Help all mothers seek your guidance, Father, in all things that concern families—from clothes to colleges and groceries to the grave. And help me *now* with my fear of separation.

SUE

❧

"For I am convinced that nothing can ever separate us from his love" (Rom. 8:38).

Some Have Come Back

Dear God:

A friend of mine almost died and then came back. Her experience reminded me of all the others who have given the same report. They all relate that it is extremely hard to come back here.

Now that doctors are able to massage the heart and give adrenaline, in a physical sense they can literally revive the dead. It seems that more and more people experience death and come back to tell about it. I guess we can't miss what we haven't known (or can't remember), but apparently a glimpse of the other side makes life here look pretty foggy and smogged up.

"Death" must be beautiful, God, with all the inexplicable, unexplainable loveliness of nature there, and the ethereal music, the vivid wondrous colors, and the sense of deep, stable, invulnerable peace. Obviously, you don't let a person stay there until his or her work here is finished.

My friend said she wanted so much to remain on the other side that when she heard the voices of earth calling her she wanted to turn and run away and stay on that level forever. So many who have "died" tell us of those they saw. Some saw people they didn't even know had died. Since the "dying" had no way of knowing these others were dead, how could these reporters "imagine" they had seen them?

God, take from me all fear of death. Through all these accounts, but most of all through my faith and belief in what your only Son has revealed through your Word, I know that death (being in paradise with you) is the "realest" experience in life.

But, God, help me to love this life, too, and to be content to be here as long as you want me to stay because there is work for me here.

All the stages of life are important to you, and so they must be important to me. You can give me the same confidence you gave Paul, and Paul knew he could be content in life or death or in whatever state he found himself. He could do this because for him to live was to live through you. It's the same with me. Stay close, and thank you.

JAYNE

❧

"Then I saw a new earth . . . and a new sky, . . . It was a glorious sight, beautiful as a bride at her wedding" (Rev. 21:1–2).

If I Should Die
Before I Wake

Father:

Your unseeing and unadvanced children surely see things wrong. From a limited point of view we catch ourselves thinking that we must cling to this lifetime because when it's over, life is over, that you're no longer with us, that we're no longer safe.

We forget that there isn't any difference. As my heart sings to me (in the words of your song) in the morning when I wake up, "Father, still, still with you," I'm sure it would be the same way if we were to die during the night. I can't imagine, Father God, when I really think of it, how we can be afraid.

Life is beautiful, trying and tiring but still beautiful. You are the reason. Without you, everything really would be hell, here or anywhere else.

We your children really have more faith than we give ourselves credit for, because even the least advanced of us still sometimes finds beauty here. This would be impossible in these temporary, tragic interludes if we

didn't know deep down in our hearts that this isn't all,
that underneath all of us are your everlasting arms.

LUCY

❧

*"The fact is that Christ did actually rise from the dead,
and has become the first of millions who will come back
to life again some day" (1 Cor. 15:20).*

Help Me to Fight
a Good Fight

Dear Father God:

Today I went to see a friend in the hospital. Father, I forget, when trouble is not with me, how much we humans are sometimes called upon to endure, how we may be troubled, and how much we may have to face.

Help me to *endure*, Father. Help me not to panic, not to be weak. Help me to put my faith in you and to know that it is enough even in trouble. The disciples of Jesus are called upon to be more than ordinarily strong. Many people couldn't do what we are asked to do. But help us have confidence that you are with us, that you brought these experiences to us, and that you can sustain us. No force, no fear, and no disappointment can stand against your power.

Father, help me realize that as one of Christ's disciples I am chosen, I am one of the strong ones. I am supposed to share that strength to help others. I am obliged to accept the assignment you have given me in order to show that your strength is sufficient. It's my duty and privilege to meet others face to face without false garments, artificial needs, or physical "hang-ups" and fear.

Make me remember when it seems tough, Father, that either I believe or I don't, either it's valid or it isn't, either you can keep me or you can't.

But I do believe! I entrust my mind to you. No other power can be strong enough to stand against you. You have come to me, and you are the source of my identity, my purpose and my security. Nothing can take it from me now or long separate me from you. There are forces for evil in the world and forces that would separate me from you, but they have no power over me.

Dear God, help me realize that nothing can happen this day that you and I can't handle.

Help me, Father God, to know how great you are and to let you free my soul from need and fear and earthly fetters so that I can truly soar. Then I will be able (you and I together) to accomplish the tasks you have assigned to me.

JAYNE

❧

"If I ride the morning winds to the farthest oceans, even there your hand will guide me, your strength will support me" (Ps. 139:9–10).

FOR THINE IS THE KINGDOM

Your Time—Not Mine!

Dear God:

Please instruct me in the constructive use of "leisure" time, knowing it is your time, not mine. Help me to know the necessity of discipline so I can take the opportunities you give to be your vessel.

God, my communication with you is not a monologue but a dialogue in which you are constantly talking to me. You speak to me in the quiet of my inner voice, in the events in which I see daily the undeniable proof of your intervention, and in the people who come to me who I know must have been sent by you.

Every day, I must accept what some people call "miracles." When I ask your help, I already have it. When I ask you a question, I already know the answer because you dwell within me.

Even though my outer consciousness may be unhappy on the deeper levels, I am happy even when I feel sorrow. I'm always joyful inside where I really live through your love.

I feel foolish, God, asking you to help about each

little thing when your help is already there. It's there, but I must be aware of it or I can't realize it in consciousness and act on it. You are able to keep that which is committed to you.

Knowing your presence can enable me to find joy in friends, in my husband, and even in the next generation. These are vast possibilities of fulfilling your will in me, as long as I live and forever.

What more is there to joy? Or to concern? There is nothing.

LUCY

❧

"There is a right time for everything:
  A time to laugh;

  . . . .

  A time to dance" (Eccles. 3:1, 4).

Work vs. Depression

Dear God:

Something has happened for which I am more and more grateful, and so I want to write it down.

I have come to an important, comforting, and strengthening concept that is giving me courage. It is supplying the assurance that I need to hold onto in my upward struggle. And that is, Father, there is great comfort in *work*.

I have found it a satisfying compensation, Father, to know, when a day is done, that it has not been wasted, though I may have suffered that day in private disturbances. If I keep working, each day I will have the satisfaction of accomplishment. I will be proud (and have been proud) that I have been able to accomplish something (in spite of me). Sometimes that is completely abstract and transcends my own private little struggle. In spite of me, or the test and trial you have allowed my interior life (or that the weaker evil spirits have managed to tantalize me with), I have disciplined myself to accomplish something for you as the result of my objective efforts in the midst of subjective turmoil. I have fulfilled the role you gave me for this day and the task that needed me. This can make (and has made) much that might have otherwise been discouraging or even despairing still worthwhile and good. To have survived when I thought I couldn't and to have surpassed my own strength in difficult circumstances even seems to cloak my efforts, tiny in themselves, with a certain divine nobility that makes up for the struggle even when it is the hardest to endure. And you know what, Father? In the midst of internal franticness, I experience joy!

Jay, my son and spiritual partner who embarked on the spiritual journey with me, says he thinks others have the same thoughts and fears but some people manage not to get so "wrapped up" in them. They have the outside discipline of *work* that *must* be done. This is great therapy.

But who has work that is more important than my commitment to you? No one.

Oh, dear Father God, help me to have the self-discipline I need to accomplish the greater task even though often those who have work to do that isn't as important have the greater outside discipline. Help me to understand that the spiritual necessity, though less apparent, is the most pressing need of all in the total context of life eternal. Help me to truly work each minute of each day so that I may earn the right to say with Kahlil Gibran in *The Prophet*, "That though in the winter, we deny our spring, yet spring reposing within us, smiles in its drowsiness and is not offended."

Help me to earn the right to have the compensation of continuing achievements which do not vary because of the lesser concerns of self, and, God, help me to learn.

Help me to earn the right to live in peace with my own seasons.

JAYNE

❧

"What does one really get from hard work? I have thought about this in connection with all the various kinds of work God has given to mankind" (Eccles. 3:9–10).

AND THE POWER
AND THE GLORY

For Faith

Dear God:

Thank you with a heart full of gratitude for the answers you've given me even in my disappointments. They make me know you are with me, and that you know better than I what is best.

I still have lots of things to learn. So, dearest Father, help me in my desire to prove to myself and to all those who know me that my joy and wonder in you are enough to always sustain me and that my experiences with you are valid and the most real events in my life. Help me, Father, to really believe that it is true—to trust you enough to find strength even in trouble, so that I cannot be upset by anything that is not of you.

My spiritual partners say: "If we have enough faith—well then, that's all that matters! You are always with us." Only just please let me know you're here even if I don't always feel conscious of it.

I know now that you can supply enough faith for anything that could possibly happen. You can fill our cups so full, just of you, that nothing can threaten us.

God, I know you're the only power strong enough to overcome evil. Help me to prove that although I am finite I am still possessed by a spark of the *infinite,* the divine. I, your littlest child, still can *prove* this to myself and to those others you have committed to my care.

When a frightening chance thought crosses my mind, please don't let me panic. I am barraged by millions of thoughts, and the negative and the fearful or faithless do not need to dominate. You are still here, and I am not *really* as weak and powerless as I think. I cannot really take myself *that* seriously, knowing what you have done for me. Help me not to hurt you or myself when it is so unnecessary because you are always right here.

I still have tough times to face—plenty of them! Yet since you've given me faith for every need, what earthly disappointment can possibly overwhelm me? Or separate me from the love of you? What happening that the world brings can discourage me too much? What hard or sad circumstances here can conceivably get me "down for the count," compared to the joy and security of my experiences with you?

Now I know that nothing can do this to me—it can never be! This is the security only you can give. The peace that is beyond earthly understanding.

Thank you.

JAYNE

"You are a good and faithful servant. You have been faithful over this small amount, so now I will give you much more" (Matt. 25:23).

For Joy

Dear God:

My greatest joy is I'm *not* afraid to trust. I refuse to shut off my mind in a safe, dull, unfeeling place where I cry, but not all my tears, and laugh, but not all my laughter. If this withdrawal is "safety and sanity," the path to "tranquil coping" (beyond feeling), if this is "fitting in," thanks, but *no thanks*. This is *not for me*. I must *live while I live*, and even more will I live as I die.

The world is *so* beautiful. ("Beautiful!" What an overused word, and yet the way I mean it, there is no other word to describe it.)

The trees clash and clap their arms in the night, sending silver-tinseled lace this way and that, and the cat meows to go out and roam.

And I feel them close by, they who are my fellow travelers and who say I am never alone on this spiritual journey and anything is possible where two or three are gathered together. I feel love and a vigil kept, even now as I write this. Something special is waiting.

Cool sheets in a warm bed and night wind blowing hard outside . . . the first chill in the autumn twilight and the smell of smoke . . . friends of my memories and the picture post cards of my mind.

So, Father God, please give me the dangerous, the hard, the tears just below the surface of my smiling face. Give me the cross, but just don't give away my capacity. Take anything else, only *give me life, and I will commit it all back to you.*

JAYNE

"At last I shall be fully satisfied; I will praise you with great joy" (Ps. 63:5).

For Gifts of Love

God:

This morning is bursting spring, and I am bursting joy! Thank you, God, for life, and thank you especially for beautiful people.

Thank you for people who courageously carry their own crosses and others' crosses as well, for all the people who are helping other people.

Thank you for people doing thoughtful and helpful things that aren't known.

Thank you most of all for people who are satisfied just to be where they are needed and do your will.

I want to be used too, God. Send me! Help me to see every small and big opportunity to be your vessel.

Help me to see beneath the sham and disguises that people wear so that I can see the inner God-made core in each person.

Help me, dear Father, to sense others' needs so I can provide what is helpful.

Through empathy, help me to put myself in my brother's place. Open my spiritual eyes to each person's uniqueness and being. You can make it come to me in the form of spiritual knowing, what he's feeling, and I can know beneath conscious knowledge and the symbol level what his heart is reaching for. With your help I can understand, by the vibrations of feeling, his needs and what sort of attitude, insights, encouragement, or actions can help him most.

Thank you for this ability because it isn't really mine. It's yours.

God, I live at home and haven't any retreat, sanctuary, parsonage, or convent. I have many other demands on my thoughts and energy and time, but couldn't it still be possible that I could be an interceder on behalf of others?

Help me to feel the vast mission of being your vessel.

JAYNE

"But we must forever give thanks to God . . . because God chose from the very first to give you salvation" (2 Thess. 2:13).

You Live in Me

Dear God:

Help me to remember that you are in me and I am in you. You dwell within me closer than my closest friend or lover or husband, or the child in my womb or the parent of my flesh, not only inside of me, but all about me. Even without any symbolic communion, the body of Christ is incomplete without me. My hands are your hands; and my blood, your blood; my feet are your feet, my mouth, your mouth; and my mind, your mind—for myself and for those you would reach. You have no other brain or hands or feet or mouth to use on earth but those in whom you dwell. You have no other way to reach or touch your other children who have wandered away and therefore can't know who they are and who need to feel your gentle touch drawing them back into the fold. Help me, Father God, to know the high and beautiful mission of my (our) life and the opportunities to be your vessel.

JAYNE

✣

"I am in the Father and the Father is in me" (John 14:10).

FOREVER

A Note to Women Who Want to Ask God's Help

We hope you'll join us in accepting the power and love God promised. We need you, and we think you need us because we can help and support one another. God promised to be close to us when we're together. We hope you'll do more than just read what we've written in our book. We want you really to use the places we've left to begin, right now, to write your own personal letters.

God bless you.

❦

"For where two or three gather together because they are mine, I will be right there among them" (Matt. 18:20).